21 ways to make money from Gaming

By Pradip Adhikari

Table of Content

Introduction 2
   History of Gaming 3
   Why Gaming? 5
   Some data about Company, eSports Player or Gaming Organization 5
WAYS TO MAKE MONEY FROM GAMING 7
   1. Streaming on Streaming platforms 7
   2. Creating YouTube content 8
   3. Selling in-game items and currency 8
   4. Building and selling mods and maps 9
   5. Developing and selling mobile games 10
   6. Creating and selling gaming merchandise 10
   7. Participating in eSports tournaments 11
   8. Offering coaching and consulting services 12
   9. Writing and selling guides and e-books 12
   10. Investing in the gaming industry 13
   11. Building and monetizing gaming communities 14
   12. Crowdfunding through platforms like Kickstarter 15
   13. Making money through affiliate marketing 15
   14. Monetizing a gaming blog or website 17
   15. Game testing and bug reporting 18
   16. Game localization and translation services 19
   17. Podcasting and creating a gaming-related podcast 19
   18. Creating and selling game-related courses or tutorials 20
   19. Creating and selling gaming-related art 21
   20. Creating and providing game related services 21
   21. and All 22
   21. Sponsorship: 23
About Author 24

Introduction

Welcome to "20 Ways to Make Money from Gaming" by Pradip Adhikari. This book is written by a gamer, for gamers, to help them turn their passion into a profitable career. In this book, you will discover a variety of ways to make money from the gaming industry, from streaming on Twitch to creating and selling mods and maps.

The gaming industry is constantly growing and evolving, providing more and more opportunities for people to make a living from their love of gaming. Whether you're a casual gamer or a hardcore enthusiast, there is a way for you to make money from gaming.

This book will take you through 20 different ways to make money from gaming, each with its own set of challenges and rewards. The methods discussed in this book are not just limited to professional players, but also for people who are passionate about gaming and want to make a career out of it.

The purpose of this book is to educate and inspire you to turn your passion for gaming into a profitable venture. So, whether you're looking for a full-time career, a side hustle, or just a way to make some extra money, this book will provide you with the information you need to get started.

History of Gaming

The history of gaming dates back to ancient civilizations, where games such as Senet, a board game played in ancient Egypt, and Mancala, a strategy game played in Africa and Asia, were popular among people.

The modern history of gaming began in the 1950s with the invention of the first commercially available video game, "Tennis for Two," which was created by physicist William Higinbotham. The game was played on an oscilloscope and was a simple tennis game where two players used knobs to control the movement of a dot representing a tennis ball.

In the 1970s, arcade games such as "Pong" and "Space Invaders" became popular and were widely available in arcades, bars, and other public spaces. The 1980s saw the introduction of home consoles such as the Atari 2600 and the Nintendo Entertainment System (NES), which brought video games into people's homes.

The 1990s was a time of significant growth for the gaming industry, with the introduction of 3D graphics and the first console with CD-ROM capability, the Sega Saturn. The release of the Sony PlayStation and the Nintendo 64 further solidified the industry, and the introduction of online gaming via consoles and PC's.

In the 2000s, mobile gaming took off with the introduction of smartphones and tablets, and online gaming, particularly massively multiplayer online role-playing games (MMORPGs) such as "World of Warcraft" and "Final Fantasy XIV" became increasingly popular.
The 2010s saw the rise of esports, with the growth of professional gaming leagues, tournaments, and streaming platforms like Twitch and YouTube. Today, the gaming industry continues to evolve, with the development of virtual reality and augmented reality technology, and the increasing prevalence of mobile gaming, as well as continued growth of esports and streaming platforms.

In recent years, the gaming industry has grown significantly in popularity and revenue. It has become a mainstream form of entertainment and is enjoyed by people of all ages and backgrounds. The rise of mobile gaming, led by the success of games like "Angry Birds" and "Candy Crush," has made gaming more accessible than ever before. The introduction of new technologies such as virtual reality and augmented reality has also led to a new wave of immersive gaming experiences.

In recent years, the industry has also seen a significant shift towards online and multiplayer games, with games like "Fortnite," "Minecraft,", "PUBG Mobile" and "Among Us" becoming some of the most popular games in the world. In addition, battle royale genre also have been popular among the gamers.

The gaming industry is also becoming more inclusive, with a focus on representation and diversity in games. This includes more diverse characters, storylines, and game developers. Today, esports is a billion-dollar industry, with major sponsorships and investments from big companies.

Why Gaming?

Let's keep it simple, Gaming can provide a variety of benefits to individuals. Some of the reasons why people choose to play games include:

1. Entertainment: Gaming can be a fun and engaging form of entertainment that allows players to immerse themselves in different worlds and experiences.

2. Stress relief: Playing games can be a way to relax and unwind, helping to reduce stress and tension.

3. Social interaction: Many games are designed to be played with others, which can be a great way to connect with friends and family and form new social connections.

4. Problem-solving and critical thinking: Many games require players to solve puzzles or make strategic decisions, which can help to improve problem-solving and critical thinking skills.

5. Cognitive development: Some studies have shown that playing games can improve cognitive function and boost brain development.

6. Competitive drive: For some people, the competitive aspect of gaming can be a source of motivation and drive, as they strive to improve their skills and beat their opponents.

7. Empathy: Some games can also provide an opportunity to understand and relate to the perspectives and experiences of others, helping to develop empathy and emotional intelligence.

8. Career opportunities: The gaming industry is a rapidly growing field, and there are many career opportunities for people with skills in game development, design, programming, art, and more.

9. Making money: This will be the topic for this book, Hold tight because you're gonna learn a lot of things about Making money from Gaming.

Some data about Company, eSports Player or Gaming Organization

1. According to a report by Newzoo, the global esports market reached $1.38 billion in 2022, with the majority of the revenue coming from advertising, sponsorships, and media rights.

2. As per the report, the Asia-Pacific region is the largest esports market, accounting for more than half of the global esports audience. North America and Europe are also significant esports markets.

3. The average salary for an esports player varies depending on the game and the player's level of skill and fame. According to a report by SuperData Research, the average salary for a professional esports player is around $60,000 per year, with some players earning well over $100,000 per year.

4. According to a report by Business Insider, the top 10 esports teams in the world by total earnings are: Team Liquid, Evil Geniuses, Astralis, Fnatic, Natus Vincere, OG, MIBR, Team Secret, Team Vitality, and PSG.LDLC.

5. The top gaming companies by revenue include Tencent, Sony, Microsoft, Apple, and Activision Blizzard. According to a report by Newzoo, Tencent is the largest gaming company in the world, with a revenue of $15.4 billion in 2019.

6. As per the report of Newzoo, the most popular esports games by global audience size are: League of Legends, Dota 2, Counter-Strike: Global Offensive, and PUBG.

7. It is estimated that by 2023 the global esports market will grow to $1.8 billion, with a CAGR of +15.7%.

8. The global esports audience is projected to reach 646 million in 2023, up from 454 million in 2019. Of these, 191 million will be esports enthusiasts and 455 million occasional viewers.

In conclusion, the esports industry is rapidly growing, with a projected market size of $1.8 billion by 2023. The Asia-Pacific region is the largest esports market and the average salary for a professional esports player is around $60,000 per year. The top esports teams and gaming companies by revenue are primarily based in North America and Europe. The most popular esports games are League of Legends, Dota 2, Counter-Strike: Global Offensive, PUBG Mobile, PUBG and Valorant

WAYS TO MAKE MONEY FROM GAMING

The gaming industry is a rapidly growing field and offers a variety of opportunities to make money from gaming. From streaming on platforms like Twitch, to creating YouTube content, to developing and selling mobile games, there are many ways to monetize your passion for gaming. In this guide, we will explore 20 different ways to make money from gaming, including the pros and cons of each method and practical tips on how to get started. Whether you're a professional gamer, a content creator, or just someone who loves playing games, there's a way for you to turn your passion into a profitable venture.

1. Streaming on Streaming platforms

Streaming on platforms like YouTube, Twitch, and Facebook is one of the most popular ways to make money from gaming. It allows gamers to broadcast their gameplay and interact with their viewers in real-time, while also earning money through sponsorships, donations, and advertising.

To start streaming, you will need a gaming PC or console, a good internet connection, and an account on a streaming platform. You will also need to have good gaming skills and be able to entertain and interact with your viewers. Building a consistent schedule and creating engaging content will help you to attract and retain viewers.

One way to monetize your streams is through sponsorships, which involve partnering with brands or companies that align with your channel or content. As a sponsored streamer, you will be paid to promote the brand's products or services during your streams. This can be done through sponsored segments, shoutouts, or product placement.

Another way to monetize your streams is through donations, which are typically made through platforms like PayPal or Venmo. Viewers can choose to donate any amount of money to support their favorite streamers. This can be a great way for streamers with a dedicated fanbase to earn extra income.

Advertising is another way to make money from streaming, with platforms like YouTube and Twitch offering monetization options for creators. By reaching a certain number of views or subscribers, creators can enable ads on their videos or streams and earn money from them.

2. Creating YouTube content

Another way to make money from gaming is by creating YouTube content. YouTube is the world's largest video-sharing platform and offers a wide range of opportunities for gamers to make money from their passion.

To start creating YouTube content, you will need a gaming PC or console, a stable internet connection, and a video recording device. You will also need to create a YouTube account and set up your channel. Once you have everything set up, you can start creating and uploading videos of your gameplay, walkthroughs, reviews, and other gaming-related content.

To monetize your channel, you can enable monetization on your videos through Google AdSense, which will display ads on your videos. As your channel grows and your audience becomes more engaged, you can also monetize your channel through sponsorships, affiliate marketing, and merchandise sales.

Another way to monetize your channel is by using YouTube's Super Chat feature where viewers can pay to have their messages highlighted in a live stream chat.

To increase your earning potential on YouTube, it's important to build a strong and dedicated audience. This can be done by creating high-quality content, engaging with your audience, and promoting your channel across social media platforms.

Creating YouTube content can be a great way to make money from gaming, but it also requires a significant investment of time and effort to build a successful channel. With the right approach and a dedicated audience, you can turn your passion for gaming into a profitable career.

3. Selling in-game items and currency

Many online games, such as World of Warcraft and RuneScape, have virtual economies where players can buy and sell virtual items and currency. These virtual items can include weapons, armor, and other equipment, as well as virtual currency, such as gold or coins.

To start selling in-game items and currency, you will need to have an account in the game and you will have to play the game to gather virtual items and currency. Once you have the items and currency, you can then sell them on marketplaces such as PlayerAuctions, Skinwallet, and Gameflip. These marketplaces act as a platform to connect buyers and sellers of virtual items and currency.

Additionally, you can also sell your in-game items and currency directly to other players through online forums or social media platforms such as Reddit and Facebook groups.

Selling in-game items and currency can be a profitable way to make money from gaming, but it does require a significant investment of time and effort. The success of this method depends on the popularity and demand of the game, as well as the rarity and value of the items and currency you are selling.

As always, it is important to be aware of the rules and regulations of the game and the marketplace you are using, as some games and platforms may prohibit the buying and selling of virtual items and currency.

4. Building and selling mods and maps

Mods, short for modifications, are user-created additions to a game that can change or add new features, gameplay mechanics, and content. Maps are similar, but they are usually focused on creating new levels or environments for players to explore.

To start building and selling mods and maps, you will need a good understanding of the game's code and a basic understanding of programming. You can use game development software such as Unity, Unreal Engine, and GameMaker Studio to create your mods and maps.

Once you have created your mod or map, you can sell it on online marketplaces such as Steam Workshop, itch.io, and GameJolt. These marketplaces act as a platform to connect creators and buyers of mods and maps. Additionally, you can also sell your mods and maps directly to other players through online forums or social media platforms such as Reddit and Facebook groups.

Building and selling mods and maps can be a profitable way to make money from gaming, but it does require a significant investment of time and effort. The success of this method depends on the popularity of the game, the quality of the mod or map, and the demand for the type of content you are creating.

As always, it is important to be aware of the rules and regulations of the game and the marketplace you are using, as some games and platforms may prohibit the creation and distribution of mods and maps.

5. Developing and selling mobile games

The mobile gaming industry is a rapidly growing market, with billions of people playing games on their smartphones and tablets.

To start developing mobile games, you will need a good understanding of game development, programming, and design. You can use game development software such as Unity, Unreal Engine, and Construct to create your games.

Once your game is completed, you can sell it on mobile app stores such as the Apple App Store, Google Play Store, and Amazon Appstore. These stores act as a platform to connect creators and buyers of mobile games. Additionally, you can also make money from in-app purchases, in-game ads, sponsorships and subscriptions.

Developing and selling mobile games can be a profitable way to make money from gaming, but it does require a significant investment of time, effort and money. The success of this method depends on the quality of the game, the demand for the type of content you are creating and the marketing strategy you use.

6. Creating and selling gaming merchandise

Another way to make money from gaming is by creating and selling gaming merchandise. This can include a wide range of items such as t-shirts, hoodies, hats, mugs, posters, and other items with designs related to popular games and gaming culture.

To start creating and selling gaming merchandise, you will need to have an understanding of graphic design and marketing. You can use design software such as Adobe Illustrator and Photoshop to create your designs. Once you have your designs ready, you can use online marketplaces such as Redbubble, Teespring, and Zazzle to print and sell your merchandise.

Additionally, you can also sell your merchandise directly to your audience through your own website or social media platforms such as Instagram and Facebook. You can also reach out to gaming events, conventions and tournaments to sell your merchandise.

Creating and selling gaming merchandise can be a profitable way to make money from gaming, but it does require a significant investment of time, effort and money. The success of this method depends on the popularity of the games or designs you are creating and the quality of the merchandise you are selling.

As always, it's important to be aware of the copyright laws and trademark laws of the games you are using in your designs, as they have strict guidelines for using their intellectual property.

7. Participating in eSports tournaments

eSports, or electronic sports, are competitive video gaming events where professional players compete against each other for cash prizes and other rewards.

To start participating in eSports tournaments, you will need to have a high level of skill in the game you are competing in and a strong understanding of the game's mechanics and strategies. You will also need to practice regularly and stay up to date with the latest developments in the game.

You can participate in online tournaments and LAN tournaments to earn money and gain experience. Online tournaments are held through platforms like Battlefy, Toornament, and Faceit, while LAN tournaments are held in physical locations.

Additionally, you can also form or join a team and participate in organized leagues and competitions such as LCS, LEC, and Overwatch League.

Participating in eSports tournaments can be a profitable way to make money from gaming, but it does require a significant investment of time and effort. The success of this method depends on the skill level of the player, the popularity of the game and the amount of prize money available in the tournament.

8. Offering coaching and consulting services

Another way to make money from gaming is by offering coaching and consulting services to other players. As a coach or consultant, you can use your knowledge and experience of the game to help others improve their skills and reach their goals.

To start offering coaching and consulting services, you will need to have a high level of skill in the game you are coaching and a strong understanding of the game's mechanics and strategies. You will also need to be able to communicate effectively and have good teaching skills.

You can offer your services on online platforms such as PlayerUp, GamersCoach, and Coach.me. These platforms connect coaches and players, allowing you to offer your services to a wide range of clients. Additionally, you can also offer your services through social media platforms such as Twitter, Instagram, and Facebook.

Offering coaching and consulting services can be a profitable way to make money from gaming, but it does require a significant investment of time and effort. The success of this method depends on the skill level of the coach, the popularity of the game and the demand for coaching services.

As always, it's important to make sure that you are providing quality services to your clients and that you are aware of any legal requirements for providing coaching and consulting services.

9. Writing and selling guides and e-books

As a guide writer, you can use your knowledge and experience of the game to help others improve their skills and reach their goals. Guides and e-books can cover a wide range of topics such as game strategies, walkthroughs, tips, and tricks.

To start writing and selling guides and e-books, you will need to have a good understanding of the game you are writing about and be able to write in a clear and concise manner. You will also need to have a basic understanding of how to format and layout an e-book.

Once your guide or e-book is completed, you can sell it on online marketplaces such as Amazon Kindle Direct Publishing, Gumroad and Sellfy. Additionally, you can also sell your guides and e-books directly to your audience through your own website or social media platforms such as Twitter and Facebook.

Writing and selling guides and e-books can be a profitable way to make money from gaming, but it does require a significant investment of time, effort and money. The success of this method depends on the quality of the guide or e-book, the popularity of the game and the demand for the type of content you are creating.

As always, it is important to be aware of the copyright laws and trademark laws of the games you are writing about, as they have strict guidelines for using their intellectual property in your guides and e-books. Additionally, it's also important to ensure that the information in your guides and e-books is accurate and up-to-date, as players rely on this information to improve their skills and gameplay.

10. Investing in the gaming industry

This can be a tough and risky option but this can make you make the heavy money from gaming.

This can include investing in gaming companies, game development studios, and game publishers.

To start investing in the gaming industry, you will need to have a good understanding of the industry and the companies within it. You will also need to have a basic understanding of investing and the stock market.

You can invest in gaming companies by buying stocks in publicly traded companies such as Activision Blizzard, Electronic Arts, and Tencent. You can also invest in smaller, privately held game development studios and publishers. Additionally, you can also invest in gaming-related startups and venture funds that focus on the gaming industry.

Investing in the gaming industry can be a profitable way to make money from gaming, but it does require a significant investment of time, effort and money. The success of this method depends on the performance of the companies and the overall health of the gaming industry.

It's important to do your due diligence and research the companies you are considering investing in, as well as the industry trends, to make informed investment decisions. Additionally, it's important to be aware of the volatility of the stock market and the risks involved in investing.

11. Building and monetizing gaming communities

Another way to make money from gaming is by building and monetizing gaming communities. This involves creating and growing a community of players around a specific game or a gaming-related topic, and then monetizing that community through various means such as advertising, sponsorships, and paid membership.

To start building and monetizing a gaming community, you will need to have a good understanding of the game or topic you are building around and be able to create and share engaging content. You will also need to be able to manage and moderate a community effectively.

You can build your community on various platforms such as Discord, Reddit, or Facebook groups. Once you have a sizable community, you can monetize it by offering advertising space, sponsorships and paid memberships. Additionally, you can also offer exclusive content and perks to members who pay for a subscription.

Building and monetizing gaming communities can be a profitable way to make money from gaming, but it does require a significant investment of time, effort and money. The success of this method depends on the size and engagement of the community, the demand for the topic, and the ability to monetize the community effectively.

It's important to be aware of the rules and guidelines of the platforms you are using and make sure you are following them. Additionally, it's also important to be transparent with your community about your monetization methods and to ensure that you are providing value to your members.

12. Crowdfunding through platforms like Kickstarter

Crowdfunding platforms such as Kickstarter to fund the development of your own game or gaming-related projects can generate a huge revenue Crowdfunding allows creators to raise money from a large number of people, usually through the internet, in order to finance a project or venture.

To start a crowdfunding campaign on Kickstarter, you will need to have a clear and compelling project idea, a detailed project plan, and a pitch video to present your project to potential backers. You will also need to create rewards and perks for backers at different funding levels.

Once your campaign is live, you will need to promote it through social media and other channels to reach potential backers. If your campaign is successful and reaches its funding goal, you will then receive the funds to develop your project. If the campaign is unsuccessful, the funds will be returned to the backers.

Crowdfunding can be a great way to raise money for your game development or gaming-related projects, but it does require a significant investment of time, effort, and money in the preparation and promotion of the campaign. The success of this method depends on the quality of your project, the strength of your pitch, and the ability to promote it effectively.

It's important to be aware of the terms and conditions of the crowdfunding platform you are using and make sure you are following them. Additionally, it's also important to be transparent with your backers about your project and the use of funds, and to provide regular updates on the progress of your project.

13. Making money through affiliate marketing

Making money through affiliate marketing is a popular and effective way to earn money from gaming. It is a performance-based marketing strategy where you promote a product or service and earn a commission for every sale or lead that you generate.

To start making money through affiliate marketing, you will need to find a product or service that is related to gaming. This can include gaming laptops, gaming chairs, gaming accessories, or even gaming-related subscription services. Once you have identified a product or service that aligns with your audience's interests, you will need to apply to the affiliate program of that product or service.

Upon acceptance, you will be given a unique affiliate link that you can share with your audience. This link will allow you to track the sales and leads generated through your promotion. You can share this link on your gaming website, blog, or social media channels. Additionally, you can also create video or written reviews of the products and share your affiliate link in the description or in the post.

It's important to only promote products that you truly believe in and that align with your audience's interests. By promoting relevant and high-quality products, you will be able to gain the trust of your audience, which will increase the chances of them making a purchase through your affiliate link.

Another way to increase your chances of success is to provide value to your audience through your content. You can create guides, tutorials, or other resources that will help them with their gaming experience. By providing value, you will be able to establish yourself as a trusted authority in the gaming industry.

One of the advantages of affiliate marketing is that it does not require a significant investment of money. You don't need to create a product or service of your own, you don't need to handle customer service, and you don't need to handle shipping or returns. All you need to do is promote the product and earn a commission for every sale.

However, it does require a significant investment of time and effort. You need to find the right products to promote, create content to promote them, and build an audience. Additionally, it's important to be aware of the rules and guidelines of the affiliate program you are using, and to follow them.

In conclusion, making money through affiliate marketing can be a great way to earn money while promoting products that are relevant to your gaming audience. However, it does require a significant investment of time and effort to promote the products effectively and find the right products to promote. By providing value to your audience through your content and promoting relevant and high-quality products, you will be able to establish yourself as a trusted authority in the gaming industry and increase your chances of success in affiliate marketing. Additionally, it's important to be transparent with your audience about your affiliate relationships and to only promote products that you truly believe in. By following these guidelines and putting in the effort, affiliate marketing can be a great way to make money from gaming.

14. Monetizing a gaming blog or website

Monetizing a gaming blog or website is a great way to make money from gaming. By creating high-quality content and building a dedicated audience, you can monetize your website through various methods such as advertising, sponsored content, and affiliate marketing.

One of the most popular ways to monetize a gaming blog or website is through advertising. You can place ads on your website through various ad networks such as Google AdSense, Media.net, and Propeller Ads. These ad networks will pay you a certain amount of money for every thousand views or clicks on the ads on your website. To maximize your earnings, you need to have a large audience and high traffic on your website.

Another way to monetize your website is through sponsored content. This involves creating content that is sponsored by a particular brand or company. For example, you can review a gaming product and get paid for it. Or you can create a sponsored post about a new game that is about to be released. Sponsored content can be a great way to earn money, but it's important to disclose the sponsored nature of the content to your audience, as it's required by the Federal Trade Commission (FTC) guidelines.

As described above, Affiliate marketing is also a great way to monetize your gaming blog or website. By promoting relevant and high-quality products, you can earn a commission for every sale or lead generated through your affiliate link. This can be a great way to earn money while promoting products that align with your audience's interests.

You can also monetize your website by offering paid memberships or subscriptions.

This can include exclusive content, perks, or other benefits for members who pay for a subscription. Additionally, you can offer merchandise or other products to your audience as well.

In conclusion, monetizing a gaming blog or website can be a great way to make money from gaming. By creating high-quality content and building a dedicated audience, you can monetize your website through various methods such as advertising, sponsored content, affiliate marketing, paid memberships, and merchandise sales. However, it does require a significant investment of time, effort, and money to create and maintain a successful gaming blog or website. It is important to consistently produce engaging and valuable content for your audience, as well as to promote your website and grow your audience. Additionally, it's important to be aware of the FTC guidelines for sponsored content and to disclose sponsored posts or reviews to your audience. Monetizing a gaming blog or website can be a great way to turn your passion for gaming into a profitable business, but it does require dedication and hard work to make it successful.

15. Game testing and bug reporting

Game testing and bug reporting is a way to make money from gaming by identifying and reporting bugs and issues in video games. Game testing is the process of evaluating a game's quality, performance, and overall player experience. Bug reporting, on the other hand, is the process of identifying and reporting issues or errors that occur during the gameplay. Both game testing and bug reporting are important steps in the game development process, as they help developers to improve the quality and user experience of their games.

To start game testing and bug reporting, you will need to have a good understanding of the game's mechanics and features. You will also need to have good attention to detail and the ability to identify and report bugs accurately. Additionally, you will need to be able to communicate effectively with the game's development team to provide detailed information about the bugs you have found.

Game testing and bug reporting can be done through various methods, such as beta testing, closed testing, or open testing. Beta testing is usually done by a small group of testers who are given access to a pre-release version of the game. Closed testing is usually done by a select group of testers who are invited by the developers to test the game. Open testing is usually done by a larger group of testers who can access the game through a public beta or demo version.

Game testing and bug reporting can be a great way to make money from gaming, as it allows you to get paid for playing and providing feedback on games. Additionally, it can be a great way to get into the game development industry, as it provides valuable experience and can help you to build a portfolio of work.

However, it does require a significant investment of time and effort. You will need to be able to play the game for extended periods of time, and be able to identify and report bugs accurately and efficiently. Additionally, you will need to be able to communicate effectively with the development team to provide detailed information about the bugs you have found.

16. Game localization and translation services

Game localization and translation services is a way to make money from gaming by translating and adapting video games for different languages and cultures. Localization is the process of adapting a game's content, graphics, and user interface to fit a specific region or language. Translation is the process of converting the game's text and dialogue from one language to another.

To start in game localization and translation, you will need to have a good understanding of the game development process and a knowledge of the target language and culture. You will also need to have experience in translation and localization, as well as knowledge of the specific tools and software used in the process.

17. Podcasting and creating a gaming-related podcast

Podcasting is a way to make money from gaming by sharing your thoughts, opinions, and insights on the world of gaming with a dedicated audience. Podcasting is an audio-based medium that allows you to create and distribute your own radio-style shows over the internet.

To start a gaming-related podcast, you will need to have a good understanding of the gaming industry and a passion for discussing and analyzing games. You will also need to have the necessary equipment such as a microphone, audio editing software, and a hosting platform to upload and distribute your podcast.

Once your podcast is set up and running, you can monetize it through various methods such as advertising, sponsorships, and donations. You can also sell merchandise or offer exclusive content to your listeners. Additionally, your podcast can also serve as a platform to promote your other gaming-related businesses or services.

Podcasting and creating a gaming-related podcast can be a great way to make money from gaming, as it allows you to share your thoughts and opinions on the industry with a dedicated audience. Additionally, it can be a great way to build a community and establish yourself as an authority in the gaming industry.

However, it does require a significant investment of time and effort. You will need to consistently produce and distribute episodes, as well as promoting your podcast to build an audience. Additionally, it's important to have a well-defined topic, format, and schedule for your podcast to maintain consistency and keep your audience engaged.

18. Creating and selling game-related courses or tutorials

Creating and selling game-related courses or tutorials is a way to make money from gaming by teaching others the skills and knowledge you possess in the industry. It involves creating a structured learning program or a series of video tutorials that cover various aspects of game development, design, programming, art, animation, or strategies. The courses can be in the form of text, videos, or interactive elements and can be offered through various platforms like Udemy, Coursera, or your own website.

To create and sell game-related courses or tutorials, one should have a deep understanding of the topic they are teaching, be able to create engaging and informative content, and have the necessary tools and software to create and distribute the courses. Additionally, it's important to have a well-defined curriculum, format, and schedule for your course to maintain consistency and keep your students engaged.

Once the courses are created, they can be sold to individuals or organizations who are interested in learning about the specific topic. The courses can be self-paced or have a set schedule, and can offer certification or completion badges to the students. Additionally, you can also offer coaching and consulting services related to your courses or tutorials.

19. Creating and selling gaming-related art

Creating and selling gaming-related art is a way to make money from gaming by using your artistic skills and creativity to create and sell artwork inspired by your favorite games. This can include anything from digital art and illustrations, to traditional art forms such as paintings, drawings, and sculptures.

To start creating and selling gaming-related art, you will need to have a good understanding of the gaming industry and a passion for creating art. Additionally, you will need to have the necessary skills and equipment, such as traditional art supplies or digital art software, to create your artwork.

Once you have created your artwork, you can sell it on a variety of online platforms such as Etsy, Society6, Redbubble, or your own website. You can also participate in gaming conventions and events, where you can display and sell your artwork in person. Additionally, you can also offer commissions for custom artwork and collaborate with game developers and publishers to create official artwork for their games.

20. Creating and providing game related services

Providing game-related services such as thumbnail design, OBS Studio or streaming software setup, and stream layout design is a great way to make money from gaming if you have the skills and expertise in these areas.

Thumbnail design is the process of creating an image that represents a video. This image is usually used as a preview and it's the first thing people see when they're browsing through videos on a platform like YouTube. By creating unique, eye-catching thumbnail designs, you can help streamers and content creators to attract more viewers to their videos.

OBS Studio and other streaming software are used to broadcast live streams on platforms like Twitch, YouTube, and Facebook. These software allow users to set up and customize their live streams, adding overlays, webcam, and other elements to enhance their stream. By providing setup and customization service, you can help streamers to improve their live stream's quality and make it more attractive to viewers.

Stream layout design is a service where you create a layout for a streamer's channel. This layout usually includes overlays, webcam frames, alerts, and other design elements that will make the streamer's channel look more professional and polished. By providing this service, you can help streamers to improve their channel's appearance, which can help to attract more viewers and followers.

To start providing these services, you will need to have a good understanding of graphic design and the software used for creating thumbnails, setting up and customizing streaming software, and stream layout design. You will also need to have a portfolio of your work that you can showcase to potential clients. You can market your services on online platforms such as Upwork , Fiverr, or your own website.

To be successful in providing these services, it's important to have a good understanding of the gaming industry and the trends in streaming and content creation. You should also be able to communicate effectively with clients and understand their needs and preferences. Furthermore, you should be able to provide high-quality work and be able to deliver it on time.

In conclusion, providing game-related services such as thumbnail design, OBS Studio or streaming software setup, and stream layout design is a great way to make money from gaming if you have the skills and expertise in these areas. By helping streamers and content creators to improve the quality and appearance of their streams and videos, you can attract more viewers and followers, which can lead to more business opportunities.

21. and All

1. Streaming on Twitch, YouTube, and other platforms
2. Creating YouTube content
3. Selling in-game items and currency

4. Building and selling mods and maps
5. Developing and selling mobile games
6. Creating and selling gaming merchandise
7. Participating in eSports tournaments
8. Offering coaching and consulting services
9. Writing and selling guides and e-books
10. Investing in the gaming industry
11. Building and monetizing gaming communities
12. Crowdfunding through platforms like Kickstarter
13. Creating and selling virtual real estate in online games
14. Making money through affiliate marketing
15. Monetizing a gaming blog or website
16. Game testing and bug reporting
17. Game localization and translation services
18. Podcasting and creating a gaming-related podcast
19. Creating and selling game-related courses or tutorials
20. Creating and selling gaming-related art
21. Sponsorship

21. Sponsorship:

A sponsorship typically involves partnering with a brand or company that aligns with your channel or content, and promoting their products or services during your streams or videos.

There are a few ways to secure sponsorships, one way is to reach out to brands or companies that align with your content and propose a partnership. This can be done by sending an email or direct message with your proposal, including your viewer count, demographics, and other relevant information about your channel or content. Alternatively, you can also work with an agency or a sponsor platform that specializes in matching creators with brands.

Another way to attract sponsorships is by building a strong and dedicated fanbase. Brands are more likely to sponsor creators with a large and engaged audience. This can be achieved by consistently creating high-quality content, promoting your channel, and interacting with your viewers.

Once you have secured a sponsorship, it is important to follow through on your agreements with the brand. This may include promoting the brand's products or services during your streams or videos, creating sponsored content, and sharing the partnership on social media.

In conclusion, earning through sponsorships is a great way to make money from gaming, particularly for streamers and content creators. Building a strong fanbase and reaching out to brands or working with agencies or sponsor platforms can help you secure sponsorships, and following through on your agreements with the brand will help to keep a good reputation and secure more sponsors in the future.

These are some of the ways to make money from gaming, however, there might be other ways as well which could be specific to an individual's expertise or the region they are in. The key is to identify your strengths and find ways to monetize them.

About Author

The author of this guide, Pradip Adhikari, is an avid gamer and an expert in the gaming industry. He has been playing games for many years and has a deep understanding of the gaming industry and the various ways to make money from gaming. He is passionate about sharing his knowledge and experience with others and helping others turn their passion for gaming into a profitable venture.

Pradip is also active on various social media platforms where he shares his knowledge, gaming tips, and updates on the latest trends in the gaming industry.

You can follow or Contact Pradip Adhikari on Social Medias:

Web: https://coderpradip.com

Email: info@coderpradip.com

Facebook : https://facebook.com/notpradip

Twitter : https://twitter.com/notpradip

LinkedIn : https://linkedin.com/in/notpradip

Instagram : https://instagram.com/notPradip

Printed in Great Britain
by Amazon